Global Change
Impact of an Ambassador

By
David K. Ewen, M.Ed.
Ewen Prime Company

Copyright © 2020, Ewen Prime Company

All rights reserved. No part of this publication may be reproduced, distributed, or transmitted in any form or by any means, including photocopying, recording, or other electronic or mechanical methods, without the prior written permission of the publisher.

ISBN: 9781655015267

Imprint: Independently published

Ewen Prime Company

Transcribed

This presentation is transcribed from a radio broadcast from David K. Ewen, M.Ed. The content is written in a conversational way as it was transcribed from audio. The original audio was for podcast distribution and written here in this presentation in a conversational way.

Book

Global Change describes the role of a civilian ambassador to the nations in the industries of business, education, and technology. David K. Ewen, M.Ed. (based in the United States) explains how his office operates in Asia, the Middle East, Europe, Russia, and South America. You'll learn about the benefits that outweigh the challenges and sacrifices that come with the responsibility of this office.

Author

David K. Ewen, M.Ed. is ambassador to the nations in the civilian sectors of business, education, and technology. As a professor of global communication and entrepreneurial studies, he shares his experiences as a business owner and entrepreneur since 1994. His style is one of teaching after having earned his master's degree in Education (M.Ed.) in 1988. David is the original founder of the New England Publishers Association and served as the first Executive Director. He toured the 7 states of New York and New England lecturing on 18 topics at 52 venues from 2004 to 2015. This was titled "The Professor Lecture Series" that ran for 11 years.

Many people ask me what I do for my work and what kind of employment I have. Well, I've been a business owner since 1994 and had started in book publishing, which later turned into a business consulting venture. Over time it has developed into a global enterprise.

Now I manage a team of 45 people internationally. We have staff that are in Asia, the middle East, Europe, Russia, and South America. What I do is different than any type of traditional employment. Instead of being focused on how I get paid, I need to focus on how 45 people get paid without the 45 people that support my business enterprise, then my business is gone.

What I do is not the kind of thing you see in a classified newspaper, job posting or an online job board. Being a United States ambassador to the nations is a responsibility that is called by the nations. The part that I do is to focus on business education and technology. As a civilian sector ambassador, I do not do anything with governments or political divides. Moreover, I am not the traditional ambassador that you hear about in the national news. The kind of ambassador

I am is the one who reaches out to the civilian population.

My clientele is business to business and they in turn serving as my support staff allow me to reach the general consumer population in the destination country. My team consists of 45 people. They are part of a crowdsourced pool of people. This team is a scalable on demand workforce. Instead of having 45 identifiable people, I have 45 positions where staff can enter and exit at any time as you would see in a crowdsourced environment. This way the staffing is scalable based on need in an on-demand sort of way.

My team is a crowdsourced, scalable on demand workforce. The four departments that consist of our team are in the departments of technology, operations, client relations and audit. The technology department allows me to reach the destination country from a distance. For example, I need to slice through firewalls. The operations department works with scheduling in the time zones of the destination country. The client relations department allows me to reach the civilian population. The audit and compliance department allow me to reach the legal aspects of what happens in a country. The audit department is the legal compliance that I need to follow when working in a destination country. My team allows me to reach the civilian population in Asia, the middle East, Europe, Russia, and South America. Instead of political divides. We focus on business startups and entrepreneurs as well as providing educational resources. We have also worked with technology.

Let me spend a moment talking about the technology that we have worked with. We partnered with a company in

Australia so that we could work on a data collection project. That data collection project helped with machine learning that's used for artificial intelligence that artificial intelligence is used for things like virtual reality or augmented reality or the combination of augmented virtual reality. It is also used in other areas of technology such as the common Google or Amazon voice assistant devices.

So again, our focus is not related to any political divide or government division, but rather it is more in the area of the civilian and entrepreneurial populations associated with business education and technology. That is why my role as a United States ambassador is not in the area of a political dignitary or government official. That is not what myself or my team does. In some ways we are an extension to the white house, although not formally but in a way that has the United States represented when we enter into other countries. My team is the face of America as it pertains to business education and technology. That being said, our global enterprise is peaceful in nature. What we do has nothing to do with tariffs or sanctions or war. The way that I enter new countries is I partner with another business that is looking for educational resources or business consulting resources. After we sign a contract and we work together, I have my team built in the area of technology, operations, client relations and audit, and then we start working with the consumer population for that regional area.

The preparation to launch export services in another country involves being acquainted with and going through a learning process of getting to know their platform and their systems and their environment. We are talking about a technical thing in nature. Every country is different and therefore every platform that I work with is different.

The similarity of the platform is it allows me to jump from my location to the destination. The end result is an audio-video feed that jumps through firewalls and the data is compressed so that the sound quality and the video quality are exceptional. We have called this AVR Jumping (Augmented Virtual Reality) because we're jumping through the boundaries that would normally stop us from a great communication. The technology is amazing. I started seeing the development of this technology turning into something really useful in the year 2015 of course it was around years earlier, but I would say that 2015 was the year that the quality and the technical infrastructure was in place.

My clients are businesses and the businesses that I work with have clients who is the general consumer population. I export services to the business who in turn place the service I provide and brings it to the consumer population. That is why when I'm doing consulting in the area of business education in technology. I reach the general consumer population with a corporate enterprise as a go-between.

My team and I are not associated with any political or government divide. We are not affiliated with any government. We are fully commercial and civilian. I work directly with the consumer population as it relates to non-governmental issues. You will never see me do anything with taxes or tariffs or sanctions or war threats. Instead, you'll see me serve as a solution provider to business executives and leaders in the education industry and supporters of technology infrastructures. To do the work that we do, we have to focus on our inspirational core values, and we stick to them for the purposes of being consistent not only over time, but among different countries. I've shared these core values in other presentations. The core values are what we call the models of excellence in an inspirational way. We focus on the key elements of motivation, organization, discipline, ethics, learning and strength to not give up. The bottles of excellence is a reminder of the tools that we use to provide encouragement and inspiration.

We use our core values of models of excellence and able to respond to the needs of our clients in a positive encouraging way. We find that our models of excellence are a good practiced way to stay consistent and follow what we are designed to do as the office of the ambassador.

As a civilian ambassador, I am not the only ambassador representing the United States, I am one of the few who have accepted a second five-year term. With that comes a greater responsibility and sacrifice. The first and second five-year terms are contractual and are among multiple commercial enterprises that we work with across different nations. There was a time I was not considering my second five-year term because of the sacrifice involved to work in multiple time zones, cultures, and multiple holiday cultures. It requires working seven long days per week. That is a sacrifice and significant over time. I do not mind at all because the benefits outweigh the sacrifice. The experiences I have are much greater than what a tourist can ever receive.

The great advantages of my role as an ambassador, is I am able to see and do things not ever possible by a visiting tourist. I am able to reach into people's hearts and know their passions as it relates to the culture they live in. You do not see that as a tourist. I see the hopes and desires of regular citizens. I see their children and their pets. I'm with them at a coffee shop or on a bus. I work with them at their office. This done is through a virtual teleportation (an advanced version of web conferencing) that we call AVR Jumping (augmented Virtual Reality). With the technology we use, we are able to be in the presence of our client and support them in the areas of business, education and technology. Our team does this seven days per week. We've been doing this since the year 2015.

Sometimes the cultural boundaries can be a challenge. That is okay. Our team knows how to recognize those boundaries. The boundaries can be caused by fear, intimidation, or jealousy. I'll say that again. fear, intimidation or jealousy. Some cultures can fear us. Some cultures can be intimidated by us or some cultures can be jealous of us. If we can recognize that this cultural boundary that we need to go over is a result of either fear, intimidation or jealousy, then we may even be able to identify some of the behaviors that go along with that.

Our team is watchful for deceptive behaviors that are done through manipulation, often done in a selfish way. I will say that again, our team looks for deceptive behavior that is done in a manipulative way caused by selfish reasons. We have to watch for this. We know the source or root of the deceptive behaviors. This comes from fear or intimidation or jealousy that root sprouts or blossoms. That behavior which can be deception cause by manipulation through selfish ways, so these are the key elements that we look for.

We do not attack back. If we can recognize and understand what is happening, then our behavior can be such that they will recognize that we are aware of it and it does not affect us. If our behavior shows that we're not effective by someone being fearful of us or intimidated by us or jealous of us, then that action stops and what is that action again? That action is that deception done through a manipulative way from a foundation of selfishness. All that will stop. Then we can start working together. That is my role as an ambassador. It is to discern and recognize and overcome. I will say that again, my job as an ambassador is to discern, recognize, and overcome. If I can do this, then the challenge of my role as an ambassador is managable. That is a good thing. After I overcome those challenges, then I can focus on the consulting or providing the export services and resources in the areas of business, education and technology. In the end, that is my responsibility.

There are a variety of ways that we do our communication to a consumer population that receive our export services. I've been talking about the primary way already. The other way is publishing books that are used as a vehicle to serve as a platform for other types of media. Our paperback books are also electronic and audio to reach a broader audience. Some of our books have gone on to become short films or TV shows that stream online. The TV show platforms we use are the OTT are over the top platforms. This way we're available not only on television but on computers and mobile devices. We have a responsibility to reach the population in a way that no one else can. Our connections are not to focus on people that we know but rather to focus on people that we don't know. That is only possible when you're reaching other nations.

After having been in 25 years as a business leader, I was able to continue on the business consulting for my second five-year term as a United States ambassador in the civilian sector. Prior to the start of the second five-year term, it was necessary to receive two international teaching certificates. This allowed me to offer and provide educational resource development. On the technology side of our office, an informal agreement was made with Harvard University to celebrate the 70th anniversary of the discovery of hydrogen in space. It was in August of 2019 that it was agreed (in writing) that in the spring of 2020 I would be able to make contact with Harvard University a second time to start a one year preparation for the 70th anniversary of the hydrogen line discovery, which would be celebrated in the spring of 2021. My father was the one who made the initial discover, so the 70th anniversary celebration is related. This discovery had international significance in the international science community, so the 70th anniversary is relevant to what we do globally and to me personally.

With all recent successes, we were able to make a commitment and agreement to move on to a second five-year term during the next five years. As the technology changes and a third or fourth term could be taken on as a challenge, but as of this presentation, it is the future. Mobile internet technology is changing as the second five-year term begins with 5G and I.O.T.

(Internet of Things) on the horizon in all nations, every year, cell phone and mobile technology changes, computer technology changes. The rapid development of gaming allows for better understanding and improvement in the areas of virtual reality and augmented reality. So much will happen. The AVR Jumping that we do now to reach the consumer population in other nations will have a greater realistic experience than before. We'll be able to have a greater direct contact than we do today with improved access and cost effectiveness. The economies of scale associated with technology distribution will make a cost-effective supply chain giving developing countries greater access to technology. We will have more people to connect with. This is true for the decades to come.

In the beginning of our five-year term, we were able to be in five countries in one day. It was a lot of work, but it was done at the end of our five first five-year term. We found that we could be in up to nine countries at the same time. Our trial run had us do five at the same time within one hour. That being said, we've seen a lot of changes just in five years. We are excited to see what will happen in the next five years. I am excited for what the future will bring.

John 10:10 (NIV) The thief comes only to steal and kill and destroy; I have come that they may have life, and have it to the full.

Galatians 5:22-23 (NIV) But the fruit of the Spirit is love, joy, peace, forbearance, kindness, goodness, faithfulness, gentleness and self-control. Against such things there is no law.

Jeremiah 29:11 (NIV) For I know the plans I have for you," declares the Lord, "plans to prosper you and not to harm you, plans to give you hope and a future.

To be successful as a civilian United States Ambassador, you must rise above those that are against you. For example, look at high level government officials and high-level organization officials such as CEOs and look at them. Notice how they rise above confrontation. They know they can't please everyone and have a strategy or a way of thinking that allows them to rise above people or organizations that are against them to be successful. It is necessary to be aware of the opposition and to do something about the situation that the opposition presents. We all must have the ability to rise above that opposition. The name of this presentation is rise above as you will learn how to rise above what is against you so that you can achieve your goals.

Subtitle, reasons you fail and your success slows. Here are some of the reasons why you might fail or see your success slowing down. Let's take a look at some of them.

A person can dream of a goal but take no action. The reason they take no action is the goal may be unrealistic. Consider the goals. Consider how it can be manifested into something that is real. Consider the time and the effort.

The inability to focus on a specific goal is due to not knowing what that goal is because the goal is not fully known. Then the journey to the destination is also not fully know. This is the reason why people can have an inability to focus on a goal. If they can clearly pinpoint specifically what the goal is, then they can prepare the strategy and the methodology to reach that goal with the strategy and the methodology, then it is possible to have a clear path to a goal.

Some goals are failed because a person may not follow through with achieving the goal. This might be due to previous failures which result in a fear of following through. If there is an awareness that the fear exists, then that fear can be canceled and no longer be an obstacle so that we Tring a goal can be followed through. Many people are against an action because of the fear of an unknown or a fear of a failure. If those people can identify the failure or the unknown and the fear that results, then it is possible to cancel them from your mind and then follow through.

By not taking responsibility for actions and waiting for someone else to solve the problem, then the goal will not be achieved. Goals become manifested with a positive outcome because someone took responsibility. Success comes with responsibility and sacrifice to take on a sacrifice. It takes responsibility.

Sometimes people are looking for support from family and friends to achieve a goal. By doing that, they sit and wait. That sitting and waiting may be a long time to achieve success. Family and friends may not be your foundation, so not having support from family and friends should not be an obstacle. We talked before about having responsibility. The responsibility comes from yourself and not your family and friends. Let that responsibility be your foundation and not your family and friends.

Too much self-analysis can slow you down. There comes a time that the thinking can only be for strategy and not self-analysis. The self-analysis can be never ending and can stop a goal from ever being manifested. Focus on the destination and the journey and eliminate the self-analysis. Do not worry about ability or skill. Worry more about strategy and destination. If you have a strategy and a methodology, then you can reach the destination.

Blaming others and looking for the guilty is not a reason to stop a goal from ever being achieved or manifested. I go back to what we talked about before relating to responsibility. There's no one to blame except yourself. If you fail, if other people are involved, it is because you allowed it. Take responsibility in the that are made. There is no other guilty person causing your failure. Other people, including family and friends can be removed from your journey so that you can achieve your destiny.

The scripture of John chapter 10 verse 10 says, the thief comes only to steal and kill and destroy. I have come that they may have, well, I forget the rest, but it says the thief comes only to steal, kill, and destroy. The thief relates to people who try to steal, kill, and destroy. So what is it that is being stolen or killed or destroyed? It is hopes, desires, prosperity, freedom, peace, love, and joy. The thief is that opponent against you who is not for you. The thief are other people or organizations that do not have you in their best interest. They are not to support you. Be aware of that

In the book of Galatians, chapter five verses 22 through 23 the fruits of the spirit aren't defined as love, joy, peace, kindness, goodness, faithfulness, gentleness, and self control.

Those fruits of the spirit are not seen in the thief that is shown in the scripture. John chapter 10 verse 10 the scripture of John 10 verse 10 says that the thief comes only to steal, kill, and destroy. That is very much different than the fruits of the spirit, as defined as love, joy, peace, kindness, goodness, faithfulness, gentleness, and self-control.

So let's talk about the difference. Let's talk about people who are derogatory or sarcastic or condemning in their words or behavior. Those kinds of people are people who are more defined as the thief as we talked about in the scripture. John chapter 10 verse 10 this kind of person or people are not what you would see in terms of the fruits of the spirit as shown in the scripture. Galatians chapter five verse 22 through 23 let's talk more about the reasons why people use derogatory words or behaviors against you or condemning words or behavior against you or sarcastic words or behavior against you.

There are three reasons why people are against you in terms of derogatory remarks, sarcastic behavior or condemning actions. These types of words, behaviors, or actions are against you and not for you. There are three categories that identify the reasons why people do this. The first one is a person can be afraid of you. The second is jealous of you. The third one is they could be intimidated by you. The easiest way to remember the reasons why people are against you are the three words, afraid, jealous, intimidated, whatever the words are, the behaviors are, it will fall into one of three categories as to the reason why people do this. If a person is derogatory in their remarks to you or sarcastic in their behavior, it is because of one or more of three things. They are afraid or jealous or intimidated by you. If you know this to be true, then you will know that the blame is not on you. You are not the one. It is the thief that is trying to kill, steal, and destroy what has been promised to you.

We will now turn our attention on how to discern the hidden patterns as to why people have derogatory words or condemning behavior against you that are on the foundation of either being afraid, jealous or intimidated by you. The hidden patterns of behavior and perhaps their choice of words comes from deception, manipulation or selfishness. A person's behavior can relate to one of deception. The way the deception is manifested is through manipulation. The reason why manipulation is done is through selfish behavior. The easiest way to remember these hidden patterns is to remember the three words, deception, manipulation, selfishness.

There are simple ways to avoid people who are against you when they deceive you through a process of manipulation based on selfishness, the first thing you can do is stop feeling guilty as the problem isn't with yourself.

The second one is to limit interaction and that's easy enough, and the third one is to avoid confrontation. You won't feel guilty if you limit the interaction, which in turn will avoid the confrontation.

The three ways to remember how to handle people of deception through their manipulative behavior for selfish reasons is to stop feeling guilty and limit the interaction which results in less confrontation.

We have talked about so far about the people to avoid such as the thief that is talked about in the scripture. John chapter 10 verse 10 where in part it reads that the thief comes only to steal and kill and destroy. Now let's turn to our attention to the opposite of the thief. Let's turn our attention to those who have characteristics of the positive. Instead of the negative.

There are three primary characteristics that show what those characteristics are like. You will notice that they have a high level of energy and I am talking about positive energy. These kinds of people have a focus of concentration because of their high energy. They are also led in their success through the faith in God's favor and provision to deliver from the yolk and burdens that this world has that is against us.

So, let me talk about those characteristics again. The first one I talked about earlier was the high level of energy which can be seen as that high bubbly, spiraling, happy person that enjoys being with people. It is this kind of person you know is not intended to steal or kill or destroy your hopes and dreams. This is especially true if you are able to discern correctly that they are not deceptive in a manipulative way due to selfish behaviors. Good people also have a focus in concentration. You notice that they know exactly what their goals and plans are either at school or at their or with their family. These are the kinds of people that know exactly what is going up. They also have a clear sense of their future and that future that they have a clear sense of is positive and uplifting. I talked before that the positive people that you want to have in your life have faith in God's favor and provision to deliver from the yolk and burdens of that which is against us in this world. These kinds of people have a Bible in their hand. They perhaps attend a church service. They understand that there's a greater power beyond themselves intended to nurture and guide them in their life. They know who God is and have a relationship with God. That is why they have favor and provision from God.

As part of my business that was launched in the year 1994, we have a set of core values that we call our *models of excellence* that can also be helpful to those who want to rise above the opposition and to succeed. These core values not only are effective for business, but they're also effective in your life. They, by no means replace that which is in the Bible. The Bible has a set of principles and teachings that are best taught by reading the Bible and attending a church service. The models of excellence that I present here in this presentation today is part of the mission statement and core values of a business. This is part of the strategy in the planning of success. It is the light that God gave me to be successful in a global international business that started in the year 1994 and flourishes today.

That being said, I will share them with you. The words to remember come from the acronym of models. Model stands for the words, motivate, organize, organize, discipline, ethics, learning and strength.

Let's talk about the first one. Motivate. You need to be motivated to go forward. To go forward.

You need to be organized. Being organized is the second one. To follow an organized path, you must be disciplined as part of being. You must have ethical behavior.

Ethical behavior relates to knowing the difference between right and wrong. The Bible teaches us the principles of what is right and wrong. The next one is learning. We live in a world of change and with that change we need to learn to adapt. Nothing stays the same. We live a life of constant learning and we must follow through with that. And the last one is strength and endurance. Strength and endurance relate to not giving up.

So I will do a review and an even greater summary during this review of what we've talked about so far. As I said before, the name of this presentation is Rise Above. What are we rising above? We are rising above that which is against us. Who is against us? It is the thief as shown in the scripture. John chapter 10 verse 10 in part the scripture, John chapter 10 verse 10 says, the thief comes only to steal and kill and destroy. So, who is the thief? The thief is trying to rob you of your success and your dreams and your hopes and your desires. The thief is also trying to still kill and destroy your hopes, your freedoms, your peace, your love and joy.

We talked about reasons why you fail for your success or perhaps why it slows in our discussion about those failures. It related to not taking responsibility of your actions. There is no one to blame. You have the power to remove the people that are an obstacle or against you. We can understand the reasons why people are against you. They could be afraid of you, jealous of you or intimidated by you. We can understand those patterns of behavior related to a deceptive behavior through manipulation, due to selfish reasons. We can arise above all of that by first stopping to feel guilty, and this is done by limiting interaction with those who are against you. By limiting interaction, we can avoid confrontation.

The people we need to spend our time with have a high level of energy and have a good focus of concentration and really know what's going on. Typically, these are the people that have faith in

God's favor and provision to deliver from the yolks and burdens of that which is in the world against us.

My purpose today was to give you an understanding of how you can rise above the obstacles that slow you down so that you can achieve your dreams and reach your goal. It is the destination that can be reached with a journey of success.

John 10:10 (NIV) The thief comes only to steal and kill and destroy; I have come that they may have life, and have it to the full.

Galatians 5:22-23 (NIV) But the fruit of the Spirit is love, joy, peace, forbearance, kindness, goodness, faithfulness, gentleness and self-control. Against such things there is no law.

Jeremiah 29:11 (NIV) For I know the plans I have for you," declares the Lord, "plans to prosper you and not to harm you, plans to give you hope and a future.

Author

David K. Ewen, M.Ed. is an ambassador to the nations in the civilian sectors of business, education, and technology. As a professor of global communication and entrepreneurial studies, he shares his experiences as a business owner and entrepreneur since 1994. His style is one of teaching after having earned his master's degree in Education (M.Ed.) in 1988. David is the original founder of the New England Publishers Association and served as the first Executive Director. He toured the 7 states of New York and New England lecturing on 18 topics at 52 venues from 2004 to 2015. This was titled

"The Professor Lecture Series" that ran for 11 years.

Book

Global Change describes the role of a civilian ambassador to the nations in the industries of business, education, and technology. David K. Ewen, M.Ed. (based in the United States) explains how his office operates in Asia, the Middle East, Europe, Russia, and South America. You'll learn about the benefits that outweigh the challenges and sacrifices that come with the responsibility of this office.

www.ingramcontent.com/pod-product-compliance
Lightning Source LLC
Chambersburg PA
CBHW070824220526
45466CB00002B/749